Anna's Friends

Color Me Love coloring book

RTBP
RAISE THE BAR
PRODUCTIONS

Hi, we are Anna's Friends, left to right

Anna (facilitator/leader), Maria (giver), Hiro (exhorter), Daniel (prophet), Sarah (teacher), Cayden (mercy), and Jesse (servant). I hope you have fun coloring some of our favorite pictures from the first four books in the Anna's Friends book series! There is a picture of us on the last page that is bigger. You can color it and put it on your wall if you want to. Have fun!!

I chose the title, *Color Me Love* because the motivational gifts are used to express God's love to others. The Anna's Friends *Color Me Love* coloring book is a fun way for you to get to know me and my friends a little better.

There are questions before each image that help you remember a little about the picture from books #1 through #4.

For more fun, there are some puzzles at the end of each section that you'll enjoy doing. All of the answers to the puzzles are at the end of the coloring book in case you need some help, but really try and find them on your own first. It's more fun that way.

And, the words in the sentences scattered throughout the *Color Me Love* coloring book can be colored too! I hope you enjoy!!

Love, Anna

You can color the letters on the next page to practice staying inside the lines if you want to.

Jesse, he's one of my friends, and my cousin too. He really likes to color. It's one of the traits of his gift of serving.

You'll get to learn more about him when I write book #6, "Jesse Can't Say No"!

Now we're going to see some pictures from book #1.

Here are some pictures from Book #1 "The Assignment"

It's the next to the last day of second grade. What's Anna doing in this picture?

1. Making a list of clothes to buy,
2. Making a list of books to read,
3. Making a list of things to do during summer vacation, or,
4. Making a list of food to stop eating.

Color Anna's clothes with her favorite colors!

Hint: grapes and grass

Why did Anna decide to stop eating bacon?

1. Because she just didn't like it,
2. Because she really likes little pigs,
3. Because she learned it's not good for your heart and can make your body sick, or,
4. Because it was a popular thing to do.

Hint: see Chapter 3

Color Anna's hair the color of the sun!

Why didn't Anna want her father to go into her bedroom?

1. She had a present for him that she didn't want him to see,
2. She had not cleaned up her room,
3. There were papers all over her desk, or,
4. She was hiding a dog she found on the street.

Hint: see Chapter 3

Color the butterflies on Anna's door some really bright colors!

Who put the lizard in Maria's book bag?

1. Was it Anna's good friend and next door neighbor, Daniel,
2. Or was it Anna's friend and cousin, Jesse,
3. Maybe it was Anna's friend, Sarah, or,
4. Could it be Anna's friend, the teaser, Hiro.

Hint: see chapter 2

Color the book bag a really fun color!

This is Hiro. He's shooting a spit ball at one of Anna's friends (and his friend too). Who was it?

1. Was it Jesse who was hit with the spit ball,
2. Or the new girl, Cayden,
3. Or the really smart girl, Sarah, or,
4. Anna's best friend, Maria?

Hint: see Chapter 1

Color Hiro's clothes and shoes to match!

Here is the answer to the question on the page before this one. Cayden is the new girl in school. Who is her daddy?

1. Mr. Riley, the mechanic,
2. Mr. Henderson, the school teacher,
3. Preacher Dan, or,
4. Mr. Hammond, the doctor?

Hint: see chapter 1

Color Cayden's clothes some fun colors!

Jesse is one of Anna's Friends.
Why is he pointing at the chalk board?

1. He got in trouble with the teacher,
2. He volunteered to help the teacher,
3. He was asked by the teacher to read the names on the board, or,
4. He stayed after school to do some homework.

Hint: see chapter 2

Color Jesse however you want to!

Whose legs and feet are sticking out from under the car?

1. Anna and her father,
2. Hiro and his uncle,
3. Sarah and her father, or,
4. Daniel and his mother.

Hint: see Chapter 4

Color the car your favorite color!

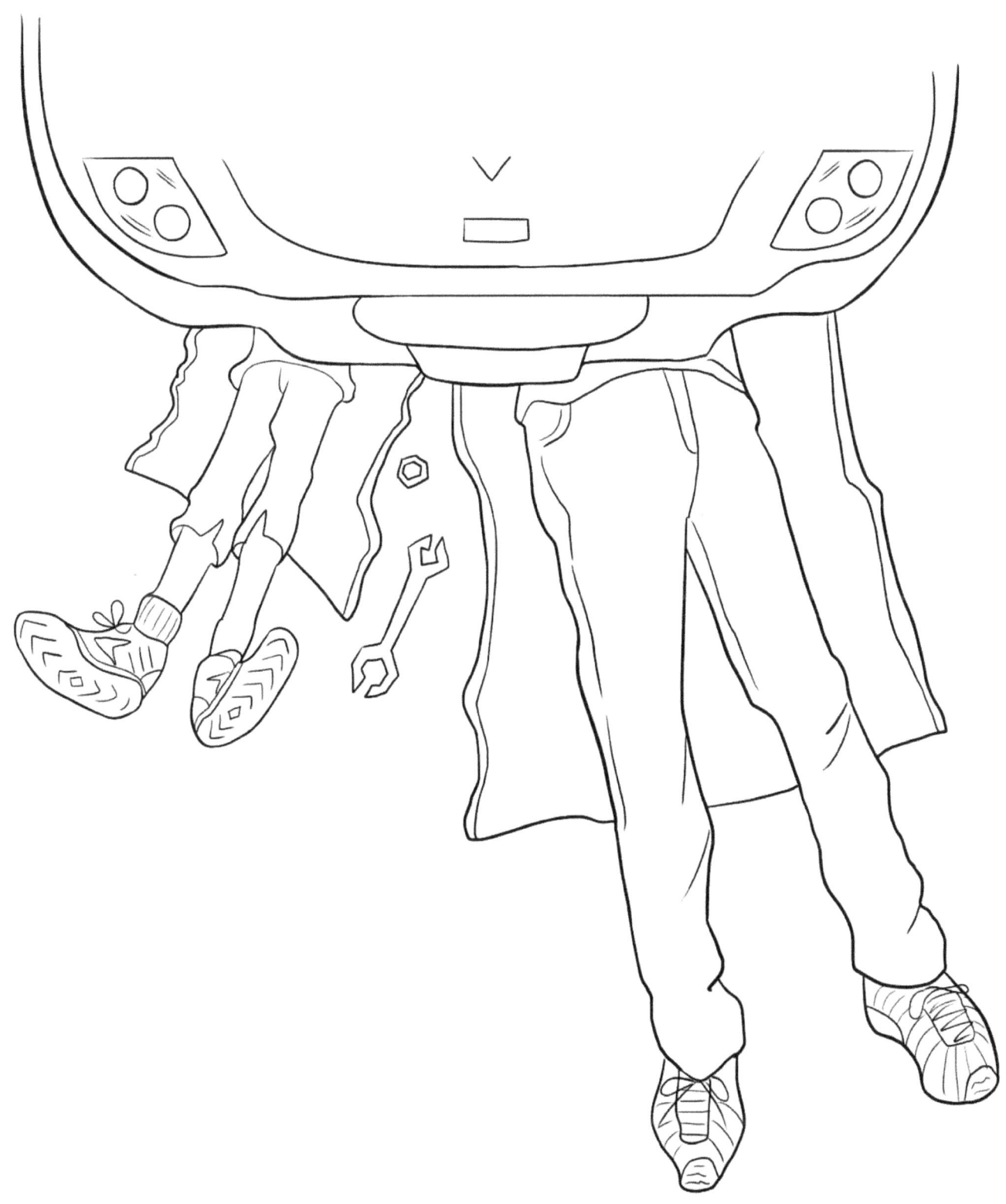

Cayden is trying to cheer up Anna after church. Why is she sad?

1. Anna got in trouble in Sunday school class,
2. Anna wanted to go to the beach but her daddy said no,
3. Daniel made her mad in Sunday school class, or,
4. No one would come to her birthday party.

Hint: see chapter 4

There's a lot to color here.
Two dresses and a car.
Add some fun designs on Cayden and Anna's dresses!

Why is Anna stepping up and crossing over the chain link fence?

1. She is trying to learn to balance,
2. She went to look for Yellow Kitty,
3. She had to take Yellow Kitty to Daniel so he could take care of him while Anna went to Oklahoma, or,
4. She was playing hide and seek with Daniel.

Hint: see chapter 7

Have fun coloring this picture.

Anna is learning to pray. What are the three things she thanks God for?

1. New clothes for school, going to Oklahoma, and her parents,
2. The food, helping the garden grow, and Yellow Kitty,
3. Sam (Anna's sister), her parents, and the food, or,
4. The food, her family, and her friends.

Hint: see Chapter 7

Have fun coloring this picture.

Anna is sick in bed.
What made her sick?

1. Food poisoning on her trip to Oklahoma,
2. The mumps,
3. A stomach virus, or,
4. A bad case of poison ivy.

Hint: see chapter 8

Have fun coloring this picture.
Anna's room is described
in chapter six.

Hiro is really good at making his friends laugh. What did he do to make Anna feel better when she was sick?

1. Told her lots of funny jokes,
2. Danced around the room acting goofy,
3. Turned on the TV and watched funny movies, or,
4. Put on a beetle costume and crawled across the floor.

Hint: see Chapter 8
There are 2 answers to this one.

Have fun coloring this picture.
Hiro's on his way up the stairs
to Anna's room to cheer her up!

Anna and her mother went shopping.
What was she looking for?

1. A new dress for Sunday school,
2. New clothes for third grade,
3. A present for her sister, Sam, or,
4. Some new blue jeans because she is outgrowing her old ones.

Hint: see chapter 9

This picture will be lots of fun to color.
Jeans don't always have to be blue!

What is Anna talking about with her father?

1. Not being able to go to Disney World,
2. Not always cleaning up her room,
3. Feeling like she is growing up because she's going into third grade, or,
4. Having to give Yellow Kitty back to his owner.

Hint: see Chapter 9

Yellow Kitty is Anna's new fur-friend. Color him the same color as his name.

Here is a fun puzzle about book #1 – *The Assignment*. The answers can be across, up, down, or diagonal. Circle the answers when you find them.

1. The 7 names of Anna and her friends and her dog:
    a. Anna
    b. Cayden
    c. Daniel
    d. Hiro
    e. Jesse
    f. Maria
    g. Sarah
2. What is the name of Anna's school teacher in Chapter 1?
3. What type of meat did Anna throw back on the plate in Chapter 3?
4. Find the name of Anna's kitten in Chapter 5?
5. What state did Anna and Jesse go to on vacation in Chapter 7?
6. What is Anna's favorite color in Chapter 6?
7. What's the nick-name of Anna's sister in Chapter 2?
8. What color is the bird Cayden is talking to in Chapter 1?

E	Y	D	T	V	S	A	R	A	H	A	P
G	E	Q	E	J	I	M	N	P	H	B	U
A	L	D	D	R	P	U	J	Y	I	X	R
N	L	M	A	Z	W	Y	E	A	R	L	P
O	O	M	N	N	R	T	S	J	O	F	L
C	W	H	N	I	N	O	S	P	C	H	E
A	K	B	E	E	M	A	E	R	A	L	H
B	I	I	D	P	N	N	M	R	K	R	C
U	T	Z	Y	O	K	L	A	H	O	M	A
R	T	E	A	V	O	S	S	C	N	L	O
W	Y	F	C	Y	M	D	A	N	I	E	L
M	R	H	E	N	D	E	R	S	O	N	A

Now we're going to see some pictures from book #2. You can color the letters any color that you want. And, remember to try and stay inside the lines. This will help you make them really pretty.

Here are some pictures from Book #2 "Anna's Friends Save the Animal Shelter"

Are you a FACILITATOR Like Anna? Color my clothes PURPLE!

Why are Anna, her father, and her mother knocking on Sam's bedroom door?

1. Sam didn't want to go to the new school,
2. They were playing hide and seek,
3. It was Sam's birthday and they wanted to surprise her with a present, or,
4. Anna wanted to apologize for calling Sam a carrot.

Hint: see Chapter 1

Draw some fun pictures on Sam's door then color them! Be creative!

What happened that made Anna and Maria fall at school?

1. A boy threw a football and it hit Anna in the back,
2. Maria slipped on a banana peel,
3. Anna fainted, or,
4. Maria wasn't looking and ran into a locker.

Hint: see Chapter 1

Color Anna's clothes the colors she mentioned in Chapter 1!

Why did Anna's father have to come and take her home from school?

1. She cheated on a test,
2. She took some food off her friend's plate at lunch,
3. She got a concussion from the fall she and Maria had, or,
4. Her momma had a car wreck.

Hint: see Chapter 2

We can see Anna's clothes better here. Color them the colors she mentions in Chapter 1!

Why is Hiro and the rest of the third grade class dancing?

1. Mr. Henderson wanted to teach the kids a new dance,
2. Hiro jumped out in the aisle to dance with the wind-up toy that Mr. Henderson brought to class so the other kids joined him,
3. Hiro had a bug in his pants, or,
4. Hiro was listening to a song on his i-pod that made him want to dance.

Hint: see chapter 2

This should be a fun picture to color!

What made Anna so excited that she burst through the front door of her house to tell her mother?

1. She got an "A" in science class,
2. Her friend Cayden was coming to visit her,
3. Her teacher, Mr. Henderson, chose her project for the class to do, or,
4. She won a prize for winning a spelling bee.

Hint: see Chapter 3

Color this picture of Anna bursting through the front door of her house!

What kind of big dog is this and what is it doing on Anna's front porch?

1. A stray that wanted some food and water,
2. Miss Stella brought the Newfoundland to Anna's planning meeting for the animal contest,
3. Her father found a German Shepard wandering in the street, or,
4. Maria brought her Collie with her to the SBS meeting.

Hint: see Chapter 4

If you run out of a brown crayon mix green and red to make brown!

Why is Anna sitting on top of her slide all alone?

1. She was tired of sliding down the slide and decided to take a break,
2. She was watching the birds chirp in the trees,
3. There was a mud puddle at the bottom of the slide and she was deciding if she should slide into it, or,
4. She was thinking about the fight she had with Sam, her sister.

Hint: see chapter 4

Color the slide a bright pretty color just for fun. Gray is boring!

Anna's family and Hiro's family both decided to get pizza on Sunday night. What did Anna and Hiro talk about?

1. Some fun ways to tease their friends,
2. How to help Hiro with his math,
3. Hiro's role in the play, A Christmas Carol, or,
4. Planning the animal contest.

Hint: see Chapter 5

Color the building a solid color or make it look like bricks!

Why wouldn't Anna and Sam talk to one another on the way home from the pizza parlor?

1. Sam wanted to sit on the right side of the seat,
2. Anna was not feeling well and didn't want to talk,
3. Sam said she wouldn't pay a penny to come to Anna's animal contest, or,
4. Anna was mad at Sam because she wouldn't let her go to church with her and Mikala.

Hint: see Chapter 5 and 6

Color Anna's shirt the same color as the one she's wearing in the last picture! It's the same night.

What question did the drama class teacher, Mrs. Nelson, ask her class to answer?

1. What kind of pictures they wanted to paint,
2. What ideas they had for the fall play,
3. Who wanted to tell a story about their summer vacation, or,
4. What ideas did the class have for making some fun crafts.

Hint: see chapter 6

Hiro is the one with his hand up.
Have fun coloring the children!

A B C D E F G H I J K L M N O P Q R S T U V W X Y Z

What is the last thing Maria does every night before she goes to bed?

1. She takes a good warm bath,
2. Brushes her teeth really clean,
3. She cleans up her room and hangs up all her clothes, or,
4. She has a conversation with her mother.

Hint: see Chapter 7

You can make Sarah's pajamas striped or polka dotted or color some flowers on them. Just have fun being creative!

Why is Cayden holding this puppy?

1. The puppy crawled up on Cayden's legs,
2. She found it wandering on the road near her house,
3. Her daddy brought the puppy home as a surprise for her, or,
4. She asked Mikey at the animal shelter if she could hold one of the puppies in the pen.

Hint: see Chapter 7

Color the puppy to look like a cuddly little bear and remember, Cayden likes polka dots on her clothes!

Why is Anna standing in front of a microphone and talking?

1. She is practicing for a play,
2. She is in a spelling bee contest,
3. She is greeting the audience at the animal contest, or,
4. She is singing a song.

Hint: see Chapter 9

Anna has on her prettiest dress. What color do you think it might be?

What made Anna and Maria so happy that they wanted to dance in circles?

1. They liked the song that was playing on the radio,
2. They were at a party and were learning to dance,
3. They just counted the money from the donations to the animal shelter, or,
4. Anna told Maria a fun secret.

Hint: see chapter 1

Remember you can color the dresses with stripes, or dots, or flowers, or butterflies!

Anna looks like she is sleeping.
Why is there a dog on her lap?

1. Anna's father adopted the dog at the animal contest,
2. Miss Stella left the contest and forgot to take the dog with her so Mr. Riley is taking him back to the shelter,
3. Her father found the dog on the side of the road and stopped to pick it up, or,
4. Anna was on her way home from the animal shelter where her father adopted the dog.

Hint: see Chapter 1

Be creative! Give the dog more hair if you want to.

Anna has been given the gift of facilitation, also known as administration or leadership. Boys and girls can have this gift. If you connect with Anna, you might have the same gift. Here are some ways you can tell. If you check 10 or more of these boxes you have a strong gift of facilitation just like Anna. Ask your mom or dad for help if you don't understand.

- ❏ I like to make lists and organize things.
- ❏ I am good at setting and meeting goals.
- ❏ I love people and like to make a lot of friends.
- ❏ I don't get my feelings hurt easily.
- ❏ I tend to make plans before asking my parents.
- ❏ I am strong willed.
- ❏ I can easily get others to do things for me.
- ❏ I make a lot of notes to myself.
- ❏ If my friends tease me it doesn't bother me much.
- ❏ I am interested in everything!
- ❏ I try and keep my room organized.
- ❏ It's hard for me to admit mistakes sometimes.
- ❏ I'm always thinking ahead.
- ❏ I tend to be good in gym class and like to be active.

Here is a fun puzzle about book #2 – *Anna's Friends Save the Animal Shelter*. The answers can be across, up, down, or diagonal. Circle the answers when you find them.

1. What vegetable did Anna tell Sam she looked like in Chapter 1?
2. Which one of Anna's friends got the class to dance in Chapter 2?
3. What flavor sucker did Anna get from Dr. Hammond in Chapter 3?
4. What is the long name of Anna's sister in Chapter 1?
5. What kind of restaurant did Anna and her family go to in Chapter 5?
6. What is the name of the drama class teacher in Chapter 6?
7. Which one of Anna's friends led a tour of the animal shelter in Chapter 7?
8. What item did Anna forget to order in Chapter 8?
9. What is the name of the dog that won the contest in Chapter 9?
10. What's the name of the preacher in Chapter 4?
11. What's the name of the dog in Chapter 4?
12. What does Anna sit on to think in her back yard in Chapter 5?
13. What is Cayden holding in Chapter 7?
14. What comes over Anna as she gets out of bed in Chapter 9?

A	G	N	W	T	T	I	O	Y	S	Z	F
H	A	C	A	R	R	O	T	P	A	A	U
D	U	I	O	O	R	P	M	P	R	Z	R
G	B	S	F	P	H	P	K	U	A	L	R
R	R	E	Q	H	Y	I	Y	P	H	M	Y
E	U	A	A	Y	F	Z	D	E	E	H	F
C	T	G	P	H	R	Z	E	D	M	H	R
A	U	O	U	E	Q	A	I	A	F	I	E
E	S	D	I	P	C	L	G	H	A	R	D
P	Y	F	M	R	S	N	E	L	S	O	N
K	L	I	P	G	D	T	R	A	N	N	M
S	A	M	A	N	T	H	A	V	R	T	O

Now we're going to see some pictures from book #3, *The Hayride*. Color these letters any color that you want. And, try and stay inside the lines like you did with the letters from book #2

Here are some pictures from book # 3 "The Hayride"

Are you a GIVER Like Maria? Color my clothes BLUE

Maria's mother is brushing her hair. Where is she getting ready to go?

1. Maria is getting ready for Sunday School,
2. Maria is getting ready to go to dinner with her mama,
3. Maria's mama is studying to be a hair dresser so she is practicing on Maria just for fun, or,
4. Maria's mama is helping her get ready to go to a party at Anna's house.

Hint: see Chapter 2

Color Maria's sweater and skirt the same color she says it is in Chapter 2!

Maria is in Sunday school. What scripture is she marking in her bible?

1. Psalms 23:1 The Lord is my shepherd I shall not want,
2. Genesis 1:1 In the beginning God created the heaven and the earth,
3. John 3:16 For God so loved the world that He gave his only son, or,
4. Matthew 25:35-36 I needed clothes and you gave me something to wear.

Hint: see chapter 2

Color Maria's clothes the same as in the previous picture!

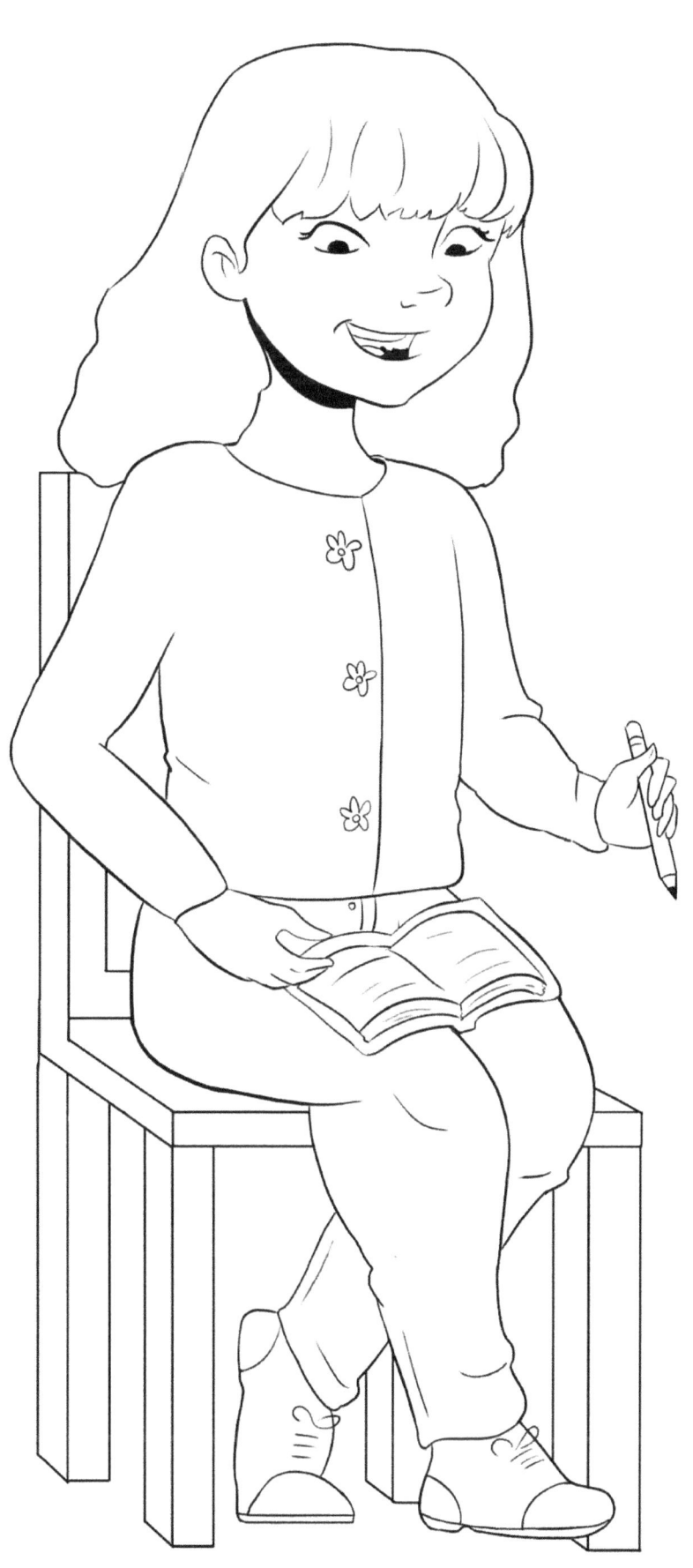

Maria came to help Cayden when she heard her yelling down the hallway at school. Why was Cayden yelling?

1. Cayden saw a big black roach crawling across the floor,
2. A bully had just cracked eggs over Cayden's head,
3. Cayden was trying to stop a fight between Jesse and Daniel, or,
4. Someone else was yelling that sounded like Cayden but it wasn't her.

Hint: see Chapter 3

The students got to dress up for Halloween Day at school. Maria is a princess and Cayden is an angel!

What are Anna, Maria and Cayden doing in the girl's bathroom?

1. They are bleaching Cayden's hair so it will match her angel costume,
2. A bully put chewing gum in Cayden's hair,
3. They are trying to wash the eggs out of Cayden's hair, or
4. They were supposed to be washing the bathroom but got carried away with the soap suds.

Hint: see chapter 3

Color the costumes! Maria is a princess, Cayden is an angel, and Anna is a hobo.

Why is Maria looking mad at the boy sitting on the bus and reading a book?

1. Maria was trying to see what book he is reading,
2. The boy was sitting in Maria's favorite seat,
3. Maria didn't know who he was and wanted to tell him hello, or,
4. The boy jumped in front of Maria and grabbed the seat before she did.

Hint: see chapter 4

Make this a really cool school bus. Color it some fun colors!

What is the boy's name that Maria is yelling at and why is she mad at him?

1. Maria is yelling at Joseph because he pushed her,
2. Cecil stuck his tongue out at Maria so she stuck hers out back and they started yelling,
3. Zack is the boy's name and Maria is yelling at him because he squashed her sandwich, or
4. The boy's name is Tom and he was bullying Cecil on the bus.

Hint: see Chapter 4

Color inside the lines. Maria has on her favorite sweat suit because it's cold!

Why were Anna and Maria sent to the Principal's Office?

1. Anna accused Maria of lying and they got in a fight,
2. Maria didn't answer Mr. Henderson when he called on her,
3. Principal Johnson asked Mr. Henderson to send them there so they could help plan a party, or
4. Maria pulled Anna's pigtails and started a fight.

Hint: see Chapter 5

Anna and Maria don't look like friends anymore. Color this some colors that make them look happier!

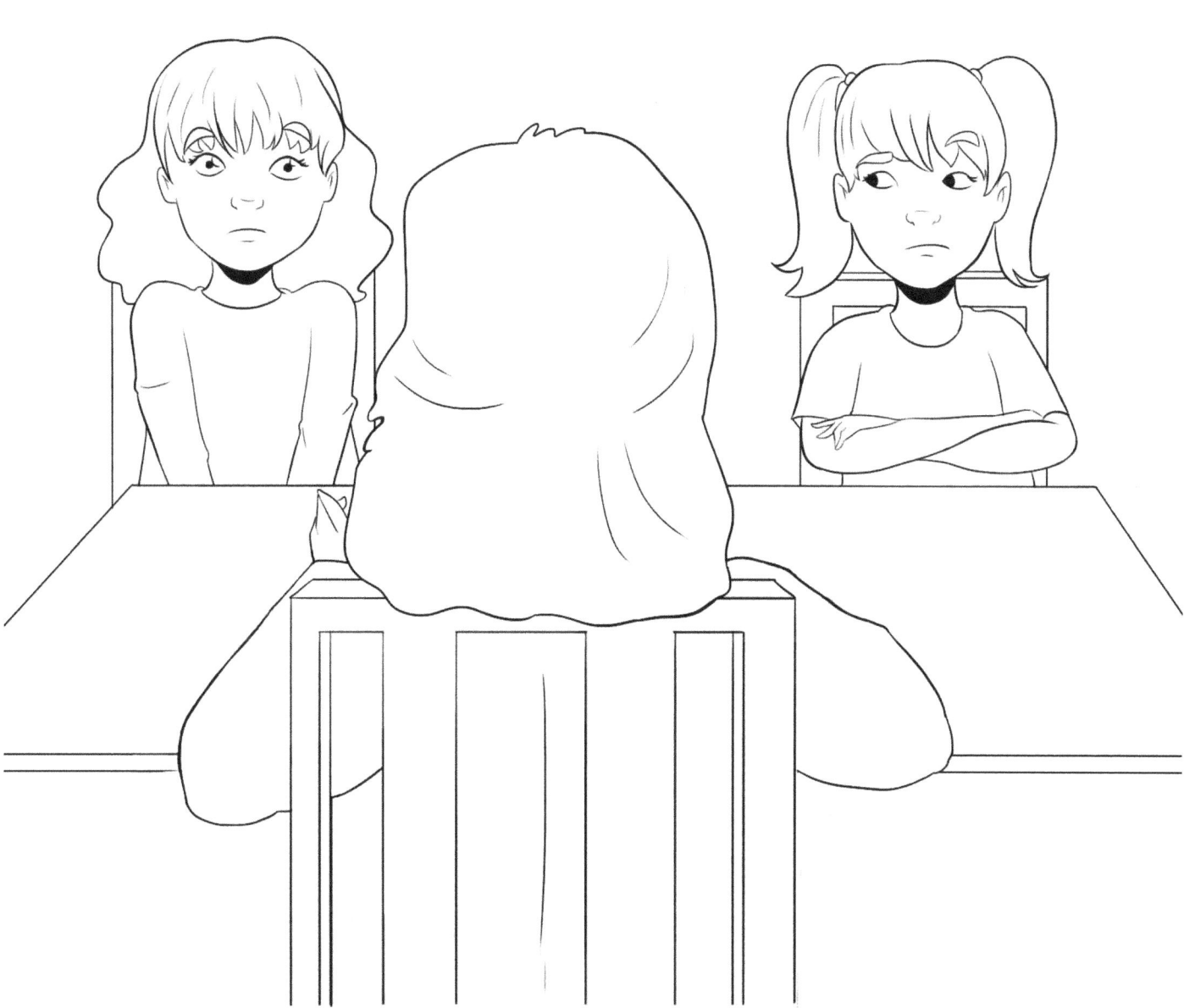

Who is this little girl and what is she doing?

1. Her name is Angela and she is running down the sidewalk chasing a cat,
2. Her name is Susie and she is playing marbles,
3. Sophia is her name and she is playing hop scotch on the sidewalk by the church, or
4. Roberta is her name and she is running after a ball.

Hint: see chapter 6

Color this little girl colors that make her happy!

Why is Maria standing at the locker and talking with Joshua?

1. Maria's locker wouldn't open and she asked him to help her get it open,
2. Maria invited him for Thanksgiving dinner at her house,
3. Maria wanted to ask Joshua to take her to the school dance, or,
4. Maria wanted to tell Joshua about the pumpkin contest and a boy pushed her and she almost ran into the locker.

Hint: see Chapter 7

Color this however you like! Lockers don't have to be gray!

Who created this pumpkin for the pumpkin contest and what did they win?

1. Hiro and Jesse, and they won second place,
2. Anna and Maria, and they won first place,
3. Sarah and Daniel who won honorable mention, or it was,
4. Cayden and Cecil who didn't win anything.

Hint: see Chapter 8

Color this pumpkin and add a ribbon that shows what place they won!

What are Anna, Maria and Furry Fred doing in the back of the truck?

1. They are going to a fall pic-nik,
2. They are going on a hayride,
3. They are going to a party at Jesse's house, or
4. They are going tric-or-treating.

Hint: see chapter 8

Color this picture like the one on The front of the book, "The Hayride

Who is the little girl that is
Sleeping on Furry Fred's tummy?

1. Maria's cousin, Danielle,
2. Hiro's little sister, Sakae,
3. Cayden's cousin, Bella, or
4. Joshua's little sister, Sophie.

Hint: see chapter 9

Color this picture like the one on
The front of the book, "The Hayride

Who is Maria asking God to come for Thanksgiving Dinner?

1. All 7 of Anna's friends,
2. Mr. Abercrombie, her Sunday school teacher,
3. Anna and her family, or,
4. Joshua, Sophie, and their momma.

Hint: see Chapter 9

Color Maria's bedspread a color that matched the daisies, maybe add some stems and leaves to them!

Find the seven different foods that are on this Thanksgiving dinner table and color them the color they should be. Also color the pretty table cloth too!

1. Mashed potatoes
2. Turkey
3. Gravy
4. Dinner roles
5. Apple
6. Cranberry sauce
7. Dressing

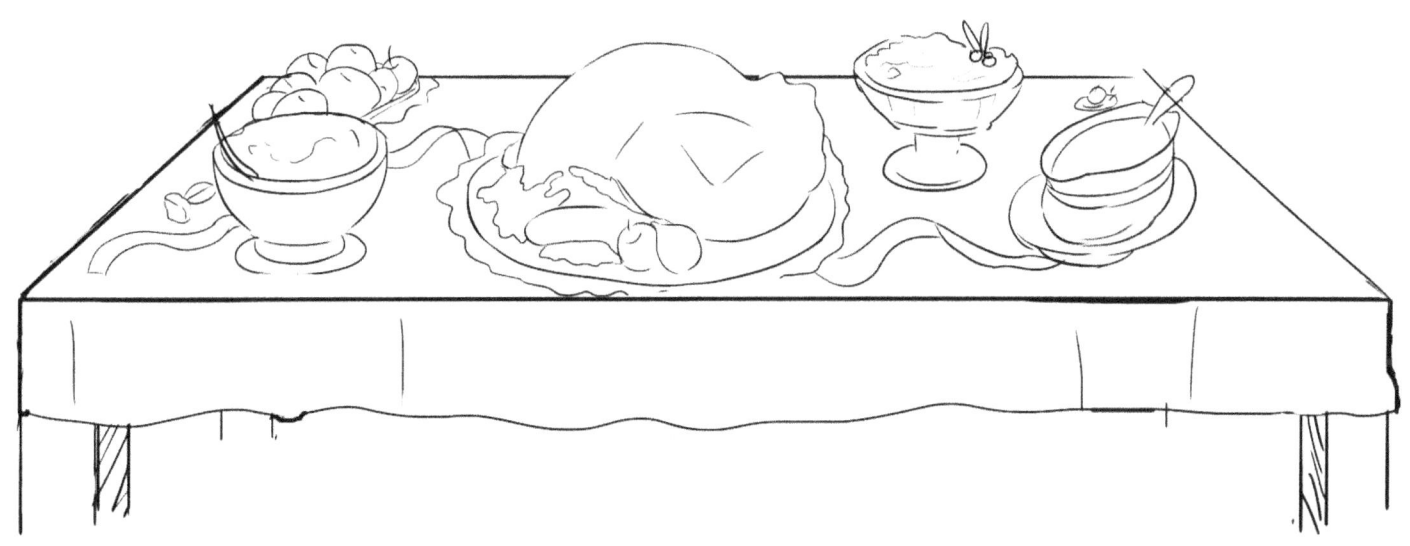

Maria is swinging on the swing in her backyard after Thanksgiving. What is she thinking about?

1. How she can't wait to bite into a good turkey sandwich and pumpkin pie,
2. Maria is thinking about Sophie and why she doesn't talk,
3. Maria is thinking about how she and Anna compete to see who swings the highest, or,
4. She is thinking about going back to school after Thanksgiving holiday.

Hint: see Chapter 2

What other color does Maria like? It was the color of her sweater on Thanksgiving day.

Maria has been given the gift of giving. Both girls and boys can have this gift. If you connected with Maria when you read book #3, *The Hayride*, you might have the same gift. Here are some ways you can tell. If you mark 10 or more of these boxes you have a strong gift of giving like Maria does. Remember to ask your mom or dad if you don't understand.

- ❑ I care deeply that people have food and clothes.
- ❑ I am responsible with my allowance and the things I have.
- ❑ I am a very supportive friend.
- ❑ I am a part of a lot of groups in school.
- ❑ I'm willing to give away my toys and other things if they can bless and help someone else.
- ❑ It hurts me to see hungry people.
- ❑ I like to earn money by doing chores and then give some of it away.
- ❑ I'm a very positive person.
- ❑ I'm very friendly to my friends and other people.
- ❑ I like to give money in the offering plate at church.
- ❑ I do not like to see others cheating.
- ❑ I don't like to see others give money for the wrong reason.
- ❑ I love a good meal.
- ❑ I would rather play with my friends than with toys.

Here is a fun puzzle about book #3 – *The Hayride*. The answers can be across, up, down, or diagonal. Circle the answers when you find them.

1. Who helped Anna and Maria count the money in Chapter 1?
2. Where is Maria going when she sees the little girl in Chapter 2?
3. What did the bully put in Cayden's hair in Chapter 3?
4. What is the name of the boy sitting in Maria's seat on the bus in Chapter 4?
5. What is the last name of the principal in Chapter 5?
6. What is the book of the bible that Maria studies in Sunday school in Chapter 6?
7. What food does Maria tell the boy at lunch to put back on the food counter in Chapter 7?
8. What contest does Anna and Maria win at the festival in Chapter 8?
9. What event do Anna and her friends go on in Chapter 9?
10. What does the janitor do a lot of that gave him his nick-name in Chapter 1?
11. What kind of fight does Mrs. Johnson have with Anna, Maria, and Cayden in the bathroom in Chapter 3?
12. What did Maria accuse Anna of doing in Chapter 5?
13. What does a student call Maria in the lunch line in Chapter 7?
14. What is the name of the flowers on Maria's bed-spread and curtains in Chapter 10?

S	E	H	H	A	Y	R	I	D	E	S	S
M	G	G	S	J	N	M	I	Y	X	L	U
I	T	D	G	O	J	O	H	N	S	O	N
L	S	A	B	S	C	V	A	P	Y	W	D
E	H	I	K	S	R	Q	Y	U	J	P	A
J	O	S	H	U	A	W	M	M	K	O	Y
S	A	Y	G	L	E	U	O	P	L	K	S
T	I	M	Y	H	B	P	D	K	Q	E	C
K	O	I	T	F	M	A	E	I	Z	E	H
O	N	T	F	N	C	O	W	N	H	K	O
G	A	P	P	L	E	S	A	U	C	E	O
M	I	S	S	S	T	E	L	L	A	L	L

Now we're going to see some pictures from book #4, *Hiro Plays Tiny Tim*. Just like in the other letters you can color these any color that you want. And remember to try and stay inside the lines like you did with the letters from books #2 and #3.

Here are some pictures from book # 4 "Hiro Plays Tiny Tim"

Are you an EXHORTER Like Hiro? He really likes the color YELLOW

Why did Nurse Weaver have to come down to the drama class to see about Hiro?

1. He was too sick to walk,
2. There were too many kids in the sick room,
3. She loves the children and liked to see their classrooms, or,
4. Hiro wouldn't go to the sick room because he didn't want Nurse Weaver to send him home.

Hint: see Chapter 2

Color the uniform Nurse Weaver is wearing some really bright colors!

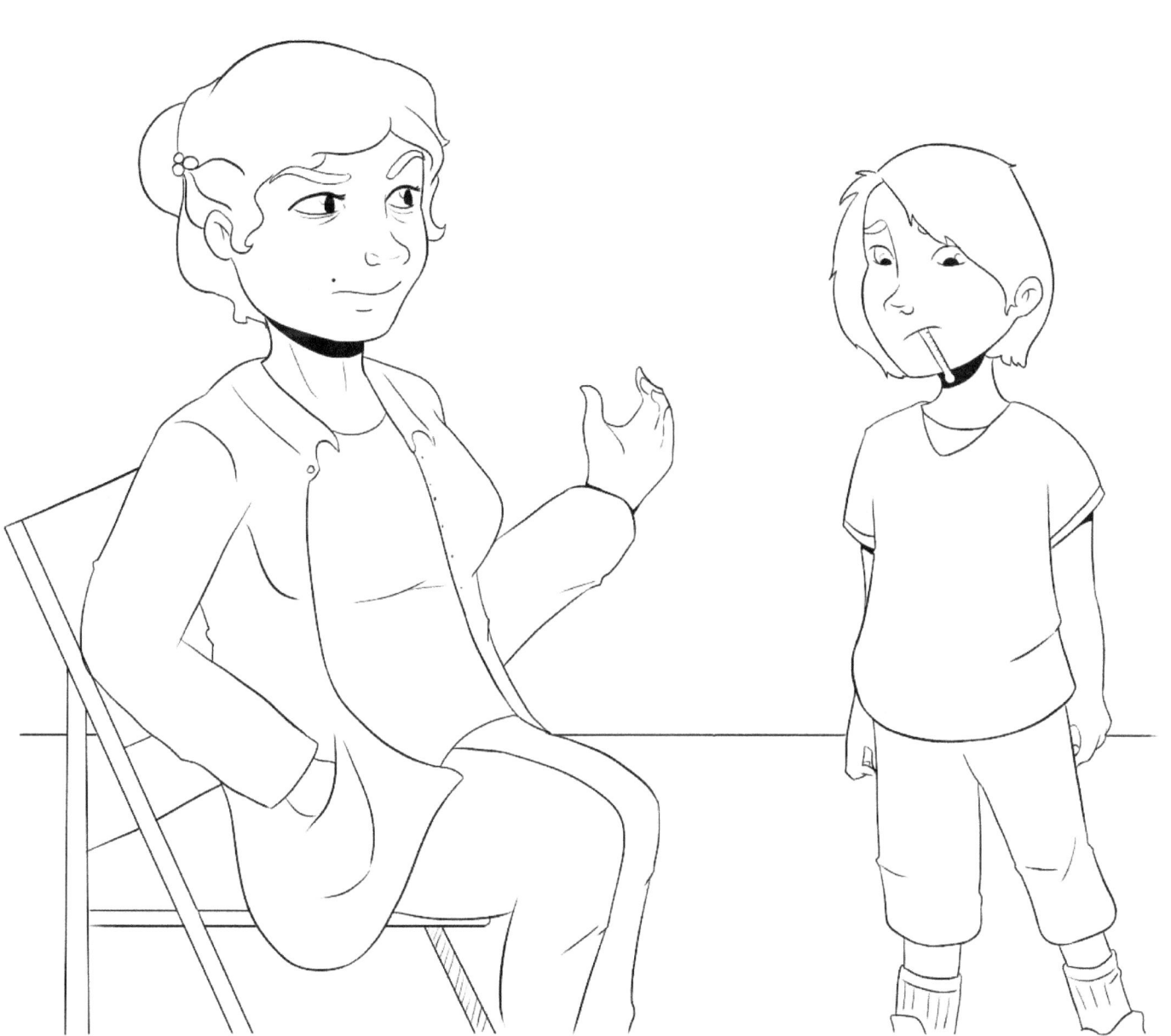

Anna is stomping a snake in the hallway at school? Why?

1. She is afraid it will get into the drama classroom,
2. She thinks the snake is going to bite her,
3. Everyone else is afraid of the snake, or,
4. Hiro threw the rubber snake on the floor as a joke, and Anna thought it was real.

Hint: see Chapter 3

Snakes come in many colors. Find one that has colors you like and make the snake look like it!

What happened to Hiro's sister, Shizyko, when he opened the bathroom door?

1. She hit her head on the wall behind the door,
2. She got her nose busted and it bled all over her pink dress,
3. Nothing. She was able to stop the door before it hit her, or,
4. She fell to the floor but didn't get hurt.

Hint: see Chapter 4

Color Shizyko's dress pink. If you don't have a pink crayon color really light red and don't press down too hard!

Why is Hiro sitting by the fireplace?

1. Hiro likes to watch the flames dance,
2. He is on stage and acting his role as Tiny Tim,
3. There were a lot of people in the house so there were no other places to sit, or,
4. The heater wasn't working so he was trying to get warm and toasty.

Hint: see chapter 5

Color the flames a pretty bright red, yellow, and orange colors! Some flames have blue colors in them.

Mr. Kawaguchi, Hiro's daddy, is playing with his daughter, Sakae. What happened to him when he threw her up in the air?

1. Sakae fell on his arm and broke it,
2. Mr. Kawaguchi dropped Sakae,
3. Mr. Kawaguchi grabbed his chest, fell to the floor and had a heart attack, or,
4. Sakae peed her pants on Mr. Kawaguchi.

Hint: see Chapter 5

Color this picture any way that makes you happy!

Who is Anna's mother calling on the phone and why is she calling them?

1. Mrs. Riley is calling the animal control because there is a skunk outside,
2. Mrs. Riley is calling the police because they heard some sounds in the bushes outside,
3. Mrs. Riley is calling the hospital to check on Mr. Kawaguchi, or
4. Anna's mother is calling the play house because Anna has not gotten home on time.

Hint: see Chapter 6

Be sure to color the pretty pictures on the wall in Anna's living room!

Why is Anna putting a vase of flowers on the night stand?

1. Sakae and Shizyko were coming to spend the night because their daddy was in the hospital,
2. Her room smelled bad because Yellow Kitty missed the litter box,
3. She got some pretty flowers for her mother and father's anniversary, or,
4. It was her birthday and her parent's gave the flowers to her.

Hint: see Chapter 6

Color the flowers pink.
They are pink roses!

Why is Hiro standing outside of Anna's bedroom wrapped in a blanket?

1. Hiro thought he was going to the guest room where his sisters were sleeping,
2. Hiro couldn't sleep so he went to talk with Anna,
3. Hiro was playing a joke on Anna and ran when she opened the door, or,
4. Hiro was trying to scare Anna.

Hint: see Chapter 7

Color the blanket with lots of pretty colors to make it feel warm and cozy! And add some pretty butterflies to Anna's bedroom door.

Hiro slid onto the bench next to Anna in the lunch room. What did she spill on her clothes?

1. Spinach,
2. Apple pie,
3. Collard greens, or,
4. Spaghetti.

Hint: see Chapter 3

Color the tiny little dots in the air the color of the food that spills on Anna's sweater!

Hiro is standing in the doorway of which class and why are there balloons hanging on the walls?

1. Math class because it is Mr. Henderson's Birthday,
2. It is the Drama Class and they gave him a surprise congratulations party for playing Tiny Tim,
3. It's his house and his family gave him a Birthday party, or
4. It is the History Class and he's helping to decorate for Halloween.

Hint: see Chapter 7

Color the balloons a lot of different colors!

There are papers flying through
The air, even a spider! What happened?

1. Anna was happy school is out for Christmas,
2. Daniel got mad at one of his friends and threw his notebook in the air,
3. Hiro put a spider in Sarah's notebook and she threw it in the air when she saw it, or,
4. Maria tossed her notebook to Anna and she missed it.

Hint: see Chapter 10

Color the paper different colors for fun. All paper does not have to be white!

Why is Anna is stepping on a spider?

1. She took the rubber spider from Hiro so he wouldn't scare anyone again,
2. It was crawling up her pants so she shook her leg and stomped it,
3. Hiro threw the fake spider at Anna to scare her, or,
4. Furry Fred saw the spider on the ground and alerted Anna.

Hint: see chapter 10

Color Anna's clothes some colors that are used during Christmas!

Why is Sophie hiding under Furry Fred?

1. She got scared of the fireworks at the Christmas caroling,
2. She thought it would be a good place to hide from Joshua,
3. Her momma was mad at her, or
4. It was really cold and Furry Fred was keeping her warm.

Hint: see chapter 10

Furry Fred already has on his winter coat. Color it a fun color for a dog his size!

Hiro has the gift of Exhortation (an encourager). If you think that you might be like Hiro take a look at this list. Remember some of his actions and character traits throughout the story and see if any of these apply to you. Girls and boys can have this fun gift. If you mark 10 or more of the boxes you probably have a strong gift of exhortation.

- ❏ I am a very high energy kid.
- ❏ I like to participate in groups, and talk a lot.
- ❏ I love to encourage my friends.
- ❏ I love to be in front of people and act or perform, or anything else.
- ❏ I like to be the center of attention, and show off.
- ❏ I like to tease and joke.
- ❏ I like animals.
- ❏ I like true and real stories on tv.
- ❏ I have a very positive nature, almost always.
- ❏ I have a really good imagination and like to talk with imaginary friends.
- ❏ I win a lot of awards.
- ❏ I like to make tasks easier, like waving a dish in the air instead of using a towel to dry it.
- ❏ If you give me a plate of cookies I want to eat them all at once and not save any.
- ❏ I'm really expressive when I talk.

Here is a fun puzzle about book #4 – *Hiro Plays Tiny Tim*. The answers can be across, up, down, or diagonal. Circle the answers as you find them.

1. What is the name of Maria's favorite Aunt in Chapter 1?
2. What is the name of the character that Hiro plays in Chapter 2?
3. What is the rubber toy that Hiro uses to tease Mrs. Nelson in Chapter 3?
4. Hiro opened the bathroom door and hit his sister in the _____ Chapter 4?
5. What did Hiro forget to take on opening night of the play in Chapter 5?
6. What did Anna spray in the guest room in Chapter 6?
7. What did Hiro wrap himself in when he went to Anna's Room in Chapter 7?
8. What did Hiro spill on Anna's sweater in Chapter 8?
9. What did Hiro put in Sarah's notebook in Chapter 9?
10. What language does Maria's mother speak a lot when she is nervous or upset in Chapter 9?
11. What is the name of the school nurse in Chapter 3?
12. What is the first name of Mr. Cratchit in the play in Chapter 5?
13. Hiro slept in Anna's _____ bag in Chapter 7.
14. What is the name of the flowers that are in the vase in Chapter 6?

E	Y	R	T	C	S	B	H	Y	K	A	J
G	E	Q	I	O	I	L	S	P	N	B	O
B	E	A	N	L	P	A	I	Y	O	X	S
A	L	N	Y	L	W	N	N	B	S	L	N
P	O	M	T	A	R	K	A	J	E	F	A
W	E	H	I	R	N	E	P	P	C	H	K
V	H	R	M	D	E	T	S	R	A	L	E
S	R	I	F	S	N	N	S	R	K	M	C
U	T	O	C	U	U	C	R	U	T	C	H
R	U	E	S	V	M	R	E	V	A	E	W
S	P	I	D	E	R	E	A	N	I	E	L
V	I	C	T	O	R	I	A	D	A	N	A

It might not be Christmas time when you read book #4 – *Hiro Plays Tiny Tim*. But that's okay. This is a pretty picture that has lots of colors in it. After you color it you can cut it out and make a Christmas card for someone you love.

E	Y	D	T	V	S	A	R	A	H	A	P
G	E	Q	E	J	I	M	N	P	H	B	U
A	L	D	D	R	P	U	J	Y	I	X	R
N	L	M	A	Z	W	Y	E	A	R	L	P
O	O	M	N	N	R	T	S	J	O	F	L
C	W	H	N	I	N	O	S	P	C	H	E
A	K	B	E	E	M	A	E	R	A	L	H
B	I	I	D	P	N	N	M	R	K	R	C
U	T	Z	Y	O	K	L	A	H	O	M	A
R	T	E	A	V	O	S	S	D	N	L	O
W	Y	F	C	Y	M	D	A	N	I	E	L
M	R	H	E	N	D	E	R	S	O	N	

Here are the answers to the puzzle for Book #1

The Assignment

A	G	N	W	T	T	I	O	Y	S	Z	F
H	A	C	A	R	R	O	T	P	A	A	U
D	U	I	O	O	R	P	M	P	R	Z	R
G	B	S	F	P	H	P	K	U	A	L	R
R	R	E	Q	H	Y	I	Y	P	H	M	Y
E	U	A	A	Y	F	Z	D	E	E	H	F
C	T	G	P	H	R	Z	E	D	M	H	R
A	U	O	U	E	Q	A	I	A	F	I	E
E	S	D	I	P	C	L	G	H	A	R	D
P	Y	F	M	R	S	N	E	L	S	O	N
K	L	I	P	G	D	T	R	A	N	N	M
S	A	M	A	N	T	H	A	V	R	T	O

Answers to puzzle about Book #2

Anna's Friends Save the Animal Shelter

S	E	H	H	A	Y	R	I	D	E	S	S
M	G	G	S	J	N	M	I	Y	X	L	U
I	T	D	G	O	J	O	H	N	S	O	N
L	S	A	B	S	C	V	A	P	Y	W	D
E	H	I	K	S	R	Q	Y	U	J	P	A
J	O	S	H	U	A	W	M	M	K	O	Y
S	A	Y	G	L	E	U	O	P	L	K	S
T	I	M	Y	H	B	P	D	K	Q	E	C
K	O	I	T	F	M	A	E	I	Z	E	H
O	N	T	F	N	C	O	W	N	H	K	O
G	A	P	P	L	E	S	A	U	C	E	O
M	I	S	S	S	T	E	L	L	A	L	L

Answers to puzzle about Book #3

The Hayride

E	Y	R	T	C	S	B	H	Y	K	A	J
G	E	Q	I	O	I	L	S	P	N	B	O
B	E	A	N	L	P	A	I	Y	O	X	S
A	L	N	Y	L	W	N	N	B	S	L	N
P	O	M	T	A	R	K	A	J	E	F	A
W	E	H	I	R	N	E	P	P	C	H	K
V	H	R	M	D	E	T	S	R	A	L	E
S	R	I	F	S	N	N	S	R	K	M	C
U	T	O	C	U	U	C	R	U	T	C	H
R	U	E	S	V	M	R	E	V	A	E	W
S	P	I	D	E	R	E	A	N	I	E	L
V	I	C	T	O	R	I	A	D	A	N	A

Answers to puzzle about Book #4

Hiro Plays Tiny Tim

This is the last picture in the book. You can cut this out when you are through coloring it and frame it. I'm glad you are one of my new friends. Let me know how you like the books!

Love, Anna

www.ingramcontent.com/pod-product-compliance
Lightning Source LLC
Chambersburg PA
CBHW081457040426
42446CB00016B/3276